sadflowerswritten

volume bloom

by: taylor mulholland

© Copyright 2025 by Taylor Mulholland

All rights reserved. No part of this publication may be reproduced, distributed, or transmitted in any form by any means, including photocopying, recording, or other electronic methods without the prior written permission of the author, except in the case of brief quotations embodied in reviews and certain other noncommercial uses permitted by copyright law. For permission requests, write to the author at the address below.

sadflowerswritten@gmail.com

Cover art & design by Taylor Mulholland

First printed January 2025

Boulder, Colorado 80301

ISBN: 979-8-218-57482-6

Printed by Lulu.com distributing

Published by Taylor Mulholland
sadflowerswritten.com

volume bloom
- sadflowerswritten -

"wild flowers don't bloom without any rain"

i've sat with my scars

the sad
the mishap
of tragic loss
or something
that was never really quite mine

                    it was never about having the physicality
                    rather, transmuting it into a way
                    humans can relate
                    anticipate
                    their feelings too

to feel is a gift,
it's one thing us humans all have in common
and to read something that you may relate to
brings us a little bit closer to harmony

for the whole world can sing.

- and that is why i'm here -

to bring you,

                    sadflowerswritten

                    using my quill for good,
                    taylor mulholland
                    xx.

"we're all just a mirror"

— the best love stories are written at 2am

january 2 2021 2:51am

i'm still waking up at 2am thinking of you
trying to remember our last conversation
it must have been on that one vacation
where you and i had an endless time
but now it's back to regular life

i try to call but you don't answer
do you even have my number saved?
it's questions like these that keep me preoccupied
with the thought of you, in my mind

you felt like home that one summer's eve
it actually wasn't summer
it was winter
your heart brought summer
i thought it was you and me

i bought the book you read
just to have the taste
of the thoughts in your mind
that i was dying so hard to chase

i thought i felt a spark
when you looked me in the eyes
but maybe it was merely a wish
a thought
a dream
i spent so long reading between the lines

i miss you so dearly
that's all i can say
trying to remember our last conversation
but it's all a blur
and now it's 230

january 6 2023 12:10am

if i think i know you
i must be mistaken
taken by your existence
the ungrounding resistance
to be next to you
it kills me inside
i miss you

i think i know you
but that's because
i think i know myself

january 15 2023 3:45am

i've gone crazy over you
but there's nothing i can do
but sit here and wait
and wait for you
to become crazy over
me too

january 15 2023 3:47am

fasting over you
the ability to wake
and not think of a single moment
of life
without you

oh the clarity
i'll never remember
after our souls touched
for the very last time

but it was also the first

january 15 2023 4:35am

the shadows of your heart
they ricochet off my chest
the more i yearn for you

the moments
the reasons
the intimate meanings
i put to your name

the memories
the feelings
i put in the treasure chest of solitude
i built for you
inside my chest

truly blessed
by your divinity
it was absolute fate
of your serenity

moments we share
moments we taste
our divine union
was ultimate fate

my heart

                                                pitter

                    patters

                              i don't remember the day
                            when i didn't write about you

january 15 2023 4:35am

my notes are filled with love letters
written with your name on it

hunger pains about your love
smitten by design
the look
the taste
the feeling of fate
it was true love
at our very first date

the curtesy of your sorrows
the shadows that i face
it was your true nature
that took me to that place

the place of surrender
the place of peace
it was everything i wanted and more
pure ecstasy

i've found myself calling
to the place i call home
but what is home
without your love
i hope to never know

the circus acts
the childish play
you bring outside of me
it's everything and more
it's divine catastrophe

january 15 2023 4:35am

the words said unspoken
the letters in my head
do you write about the love we share
do you dare
to go there
or is it just me
completely blinded
by our love internally

internally blinded
open minded
stubborn and free
those are all the words

i have for you
○   from me

january 25 2023 2:51am

it's a heart break
the way you suffocate
on this cast iron stake
that you simply made

for love to take
this painful break
it's only you
to control this fate

i lay awake
to contemplate
all the times
you'll never say

that you love me crazy
or that you think i'm great
because what i'm feeling
is a love mistake

                              it's the poetry i make
                              that brings me faith
                              that this love mistake
                              was heaven's fate

                              because with out you now
                              sounds like a loveless howl
                              in the shadow of vow
                              to the endless bow

                              the bow of faith
                              it took me to make
                              this world's greatest
                              love mistake

january 25 2023 2:52am

i was blinded by your love
deprived from your ecstasy
was it love at first sight
or you just sitting next to me

the thought of you now
makes me cringe
but maybe that's just
all apart of it

the journey of twins
set from a flame
since the day that i met you
i only have our soul to blame

for feeling this angst
from creating this art
shot from the arrow
straight through my heart

it's you that i've longed for
my entire life's path
but this distance is agony…
waiting for our love to clash

xx

january 27 2023 3:07am

it's the 2am misery
that makes our love
such a mystery
it's always the time that i wake
dreaming of us
and our fate

the 2am love songs
pour out of me softly
it's when i wake up
and you're not apart of me

                    i'll lay awake
                 and dream tonight
            of when our flames kiss
                   will feel alright

because nothing good happens
before the 2am misery
it's never a good place
for love's fate
or destiny

           so when i wake up and roll over
             and check my phone in this order
                     i can't help but dream
                about that time in october…

that reminds me

                         i'm sleeping alone

so when i wake up and roll over
at this 2am order
time stops

                    and i'm back in october

that reminds me

              why i keep falling back to sleep

january 27 2023 2:48am

always up 40 mins past you
it seems like it's always
a quarter past two
where i miss the chance
to speak to you

i go to bed early
you go to bed late
so it's never a good time
a quarter past 8

it's 2am
where time feels infinite
all the creatives are up
by no coincidence

but every time
i have you on my mind
i check to see
you're fast back asleep

time doesn't exist
time seems to persist
every time i reach out!
it's your demons who resist

because all the best love poems
are written past two
that's the only time
i'm dreaming of you

           that's the only time
          my heart can have you

january 30 2023 2:31am

    these words are a portal to your heart
    arranged in the most perfect way

i arrange these letters
into a portal for your heart
arranged in the most perfect way
to feel your touch
when you're away

it's the matter of how hard i try
to arrange these letter
into a sequence of feelings
of how you feel
when you're on my mind

the sequence of feelings i choose to expose
arranged in a way
to help you feel the most
sensations caused
ricochet from my heart
in these sequence of letters
straight from cupid's dart

the sequence of letters
i choose to write with your name
are the same sequence of letters
i use to write to escape

but the difference of these sequence of letters
is that one compiles death's date
and the other
is a portal to love's fate

january 30 2023 2:31am

i feel your presence
in the portals of my dreams
it seems to be the only place
you let our love to be

because when it comes to real life
it's only you
in my mind
these portals of fate
are the only way
to feel your love's presence

and without these
portals of dreams
i don't know
where i'd choose to be

because without your love
without your portal of faith
this life
feels like
a hopeless
barren place
where i choose
to escape

i place these letters in a sequence
in an order
with the most common sense
to share my feelings
my nonsense
of how i love you

january 30 2023 2:31am

a portal to our love
a portal to our fate
i use these words
to arrange a date
of where we'll meet next
on this earth plane

the problem with
the sequence of letters
is that
it would only get better
if you read them
instead
they stay in my head
the sequence of letters
left
unread

with the words left unsaid
the letters unread
these sequence of feelings
left in my head

i wrote you this poem
of our lives meant to be
using a sequence of letters
but it's not what you see

because it's 2am
and you're fast asleep

                    so even if i wanted to sing
                i doubt you'd be able to hear me

january 30 2023 2:31am

you're too cynical
too easily jaded
about life's true love
you act like you hate it

you swallow your feelings
because they're too hard to feel
you act like you don't know
what it is to feel real

you swallow your feelings
because you're too shallow
too shallow to admit
love's deathly howl

the howl of fate
of a love destined date
of when our love first employed
on this earth plane void

but because you're too cynical
you make love pivot at the typical
crutch to keep moving
even tho
it would be so good
to have our love explode
love fusing

                                                    goodnight

february 13 2023 5:16am

the disrespect
of words left unsaid
the assumptions
made up in my head

the disillusion
of the conclusion
i made up
of my own choosing

of what i thought was right
on that friday night
that you'd stay
but forget those days

because in the end
it was just a bend
of what you had chosen
left my heart
purely broken

                            was it all a lie?
                       or were you just a guy
                          words left unsaid
                           stuck in my head

                           i miss you so much
                the pain of a fresh break up
                   but the truth is so loud
               our love was never sold out

          the daggers stabbed in my own heart
              each one of them twice as loud
                it was worth every shot boy
           until the day god called me out

february 13 2023 5:16am

but i can't get you offline
i think about you all the damn time
it's the thoughts creeping in my head
the thought of you laying in my bed

but you forgot who i am now
all the day dreams are about how
you were in my arms at one point
but you were just a game love destroyed

my love
where are you right now
my thoughts leave me weak
at the knees
for simplicity
of what you could be
but in my head
you're in my bed
the thought of you
from all the clues
leaves my heart
this shining blue
but from what i know
from all the post
is that your favorite color
is black

february 13 2023 5:16am

my heart draped
in a shiny blue cape
of the lust you left
on that one doorstep

but what i realized
they were all lies
left from a boy
who spoke purely noise

because in the end
the words left unsaid
it was clear as day
i should not have stayed

so deep in thought
that you were the cause
of these unkept feelings
that were quite uneasy

i wish you the best
in summers end
even though
my heart broken and bent

because in the end
the words left unsaid
showed me that
your favorite color's black

                                  i dropped my heart in gold for you

february 13 2023 5:16am

the poetry in my head
makes all the right sense
it's when i get it on paper
that makes me seem crazier

but what i realized
that they were all love drunk lies
made up for poetry
that you'll never even read

you walked into my life
at the perfect time
a journey so real
of a blood fate deal

you lit me right up
of all the right love
i was seeking for someone else
i found in myself

all it took was you
that month before june
when you walked through that door
the thoughts started to pour

because finding your twin flame
makes your fire
insane
the channeling was so real
a contract signed deal

because of you

    i found my purpose,

                            thank you for the poetry.

march 3 2023 2:09am

maybe you're not around
and just in my head
what will it take
to get you in my bed

and out of my heart
where it seems your only place to be
what if this matrix
won't allow us to see

to see our souls evolution
through lifetimes of trial
the windows of darkness
the shattering of denial

denial of hope
that our hearts meant to be
together in this lifetime
our souls destiny

march 5 2023 3:05am

is this what it's like to be in love?
absolutely distraught
by not being enough

ignored to the core
it's like i'm such a bore
nervous for the day
i can't afford
this feeling anymore

love struck is a sickness
the sickest of them all
distraught by the feeling
of not being enough

the days come and haunt me
will you ever want me?
the feeling is maddening
will you ever have me,
in your mind again
the thoughts are a sin
oh heaven above me
hell's starting to want me

this love struck of a feeling
it's starting to please me
up in my head again
making me sick
such a blessing,

                                      because i'm writing again

march 5 2023 3:05am

you awakened my subconscious
made my life super conscious
i feel worthy again
like my life has meaning
and i can start believing

that my head's clear again
for my feelings are free
to write these lyrics
down on my knees

because i'm writing again
these thoughts down again
the feelings of agony
about you just for the win

it's like from heaven above
the feelings just aren't enough
to make my head spin again
you must be such a good win

but you don't even care
and you don't even stare
at your phone like i do
waiting for you to pursue

i'm left such a bore
to feelings ignored
without you in my life
i think i'd rather die

march 5 2023 3:05am

even though there's death in my eyes
the feeling of not having my
my dear you
you're my heaven's blue

but hell's sure to take over
when i'm ignored for exposure
your thoughts they won't take me in
it's like heaven won't win

because i'm just a heavenly girl
a life
such a beautiful world
but because of my grin
it's the girl you don't miss

because you're a devilish boy
so cynically poised
death all around you
and heaven sure hounds you

because i'll never win
with this heavenly grin
because you're a devilish boy
who wants cynical toys…

march 15 2023 1:44am

broken by the parts of you
abandoned by the sought of june
the month after i met you
my soul was changed

and now you're lost inside my brain
the only reason i remain
lost inside this crazy mess
of you stuck inside my head

because i'm broken by the lost of you
tormented by the thought of june
the month after i met you
when i let you go

i let you go
i didn't know
you'd come back
you see

i trust in fate
a destine way
i put me first
but now it's worse

because i got a taste
of this stupid fate
you left in my head
the words you said

and now i'm holding tight
of this thought of sight
of us together
oh but this weather

march 15 2023 1:44am

it's a drowning sight
of you in mind
and to pour it twice
you did me right

in a way of seeing
through all this being
that i'm broken by
my heart inside

this crumbling fate
brought by destine's day
the only why
is when it will die

the separation phase
it's a fucked up maze
of me chasing you
and you running too

to an empty land
of all this man
you have hidden
the fruit forbidden

this evil mess
i can't undress
the fruit so sweet
i'll have to eat

but i can't inside
or i must die
by the thought of you
and that month in june

march 15 2023 1:44am

when i let you go
and for heaven's know
it was the fucked up fate
that brought you back
this day….

march 17 2023 1:12am

this pain you hold over my chest
dangling like a necklace
it burdens deep in my soul
you have my heart
on a choke hold

i feel your emotions deep
even when you're not beside me
my soul yearns for your love
but your soul
yearns for none

i can feel the pain you cause for yourself
known by no one else
but me inside
because our souls split in two
it's the curse of it all
the curse that runs so deep in my blood
my veins thicken with agony's touch

i ache
i ache staring at the door
waiting for you to walk in
silly me to think
you'd even consider

            and this pain i hold in my heart is not mine
                                it's yours inside
                        and i want you all mine
                          but until you stand up
                        to your true masculine rise
                              i must let you go
            and let you figure it all to yourself,

march 17 2023 1:12am

waiting for you again
it's like waiting for the storm to win
it comes with no end
because of the chase
and the come of send

the send off to your life
holding me
with your throw of knife
you're like a stranger
in the night

held by your pajama game
you're driving me insane
up until the sunrise
with you all night
on my mind

the agony on my brain
your tattoos drive me insane
without you i'm lost again
because of this love drunk nonsense

i let you go in fear of losing you
the game of this soul in two
drives me to the conquest
of finding love on earth
oh this sticky mess

never trusting the mistakes
always causing them to fade
my mind will split in two
until the day our souls to bloom —

march 17 2023 1:12am

all these poems in my head
has got you to undress
all the sticky thoughts inside
and the poems in your mind

i wonder if you write
about all these crazy times
of our separation phase
or if it's just me and my brain

march 25 2023 2:37am

incredibly pleased
with me
down on my knees
begging for you to stay
oh the symptoms
will they go away

march 27 2023 4:15am

i think of you all the time
dressed in black
dressed in white
my pseudo match

my creative play
comes out when you choose to stay
you match my playful ways
it has me in daze
i want you all the time
my pseudo boy

you create a feeling of safety
bliss
it draws me in
to fate's kiss
dropped from heaven
fallen upward
to the pseudo kingdom
of a thousand butlers

to each serve
a certain type of love
of love's fate
and true discernment

i write these words
in terms of good
that one day i
will soon to know

if this fate is real
or if it's agony's touch
if it's pseudo comfort
or a fucked up song

march 27 2023 4:15am

a way of coping
from all this hate
is to write these poems
at the dawn of escape

when the veil is the thinnest
is when i
like to channel our love
from time to time

but every time
i open these notes
it seems that i
am drawn to know

if it's just my heart
that chooses to pull
these lyrics of love
from heaven's chords

or if it's channeled so deep
in my heart's desire
that these words come up
like a love song fire

you seem to enjoy
the simple days
where we'd flirt and play
until we're in a haze

scared to touch
on a human level
because it's all too real
and quite the upheaval

march 27 2023 4:15am

but it seems you're ready
to take the next steps
in finding our
pseudo comfort hex

oh i can't wait
until the day
i have your hand
thank destiny
honor our fate

because damn it was hard
the hardest battle
i ever chose
on this love sick saddle

these 2am poems
will always be my favorite
because it's when i channeled you
it's when i felt famous

famous of your love
i could feel it so potent
even in the days
i never spoke it

it was inside of me
this entire time
you lit me inside
like a candle from divine

and thank god oh heavens
for my intuitive hunches
of following you
in a 3D fuck fest

march 27 2023 4:15am

because if it wasn't for the game
we signed up to play
i'm not sure
we would have this day

when our love came to fruition
oh so grand
it was the love sick fate
i could never understand

because it left me sick
my heart a mess
but it was all a slow burn
i am truly blessed

this slow burn of mine
that was
in destiny's time
the love song of the century

and what a love song of mine 🖤

april 17 2023 5:28am

the broken parts of you
highlight everything about me
it wasn't until our love
i watched the fire in me start to see

see the right of day
the night turn grey
the crystal haze
the fucked up days

the burning passion
of these written sayings
the endless nights
of lucid dreaming

it wasn't until you
that i surely still got to see
the broken parts of me
that highlight our souls pure ecstasy

because without these broken parts
we wouldn't have our hearts
because what drives you crazy
keeps me wanting more

more of the broken
more of the craze
more of the fucked up
the fucked up kind of days

because the broken parts of you
highlight everything about me
and the broken parts of me
are everything you quite see

april 17 2023 5:28am

i understand our love
it brings me patience
because without you
i wouldn't have this, face it

our love was built on lessons
the kind of messages
that were sent from above
on moon lit crystal doves

because the broken parts of you
are the broken parts in me
and our love
was divine
date
destiny

because you
i wouldn't be the same
i'd still be
the fucked up kind of craze

and i even miss the days
of my fucked up kind of craze
because it was the adrenaline
that kept me diving in

diving into our love
diving into sin
it was the acts of stupidity
that kept me falling in

creating resistance
creativity for days

april 17 2023 5:28am

it wasn't until this stupid contract
i found my fucked up craze

and this fucked up kind of craze
makes me want to stay
because the creative in me
could write for days

because the broken parts in you
are the broken parts in me
and if it wasn't for our love
i wouldn't have been able to see

i'm thankful
oh so grateful
of this stupid fucking contract
this stupid fucking contract
that i'd sign
with my blood dripped name

because nothing about it
is everything about it
and everything about it
is nothing i doubt it

because it was meant to be
i was meant to see
the fucked up parts
of you and me

and now i'm tired
i must sleep
because these broken parts
are nothing easy to see

goodnight

may 6 2023 3:18am

it's the perfect escape
you
me
all our mistakes

                                running at the door
                                it's all i ever wanted
                                making me want you more
                                knowing you're imperfect
                                guiding me insane
                                with all your imperfections
                                it's the beautiful mistake
                                of all your perfect ways
                                that is driving me insane

making me realize
that all the lies
were the butterflies
that kept me sane
that kept me to stay
in the everlasting way

                                feed me more
                                tell me it's okay
                                tell me all the ways
                                of your beautiful mistakes
                                because in everlasting ways
                                it makes me want to stay
                                in no sense at all
                                it swept me away

to the perfect escape
in all the wrong ways
causing me to stay

                                it's the colorful mistakes
                                the mystery of ways
                                of sweeping me away
                                with your beautiful mistakes

august 11 2023 4:44am

i've been looking at the seasons
looking at the reasons
to come alive
to come alive

drink the bottle broken reasons
the cake from the last season
to come alive
to come alive

the future of the last season
broke the mold for all the reasons
to come alive
to come alive

the journey of the past season
made a hundred different reasons
to come alive
to come alive

the fruit of the last season
just one of life's good reasons
to come alive
to come alive

december 30 2022 6:02am

please
start listening to my song
because everything is wrong
with me

i now know which union for the season
but divine knows more reasons
to keep me guessing for the season
oh what a season

this is a co creative process
where the money is no object
just energy
it's for the best of me

it's creatives that will do it
from the land
the sea
the movement
in my soul that i must listen
the universe speaks no different
i must listen

the ocean the rain
the one thousand of pains
i feel for you
oh what can i do

you're the land the sea the ocean
stupid me drank the love potion
and what about you
what can you even do

december 30 2022 6:02am

i think about you all the time
it's the reason
i'm so crazy
about this divine
but you're not even mine

it's the trust
the wish
of the universal kiss
i want to feel
is any of this real

the sleep
the dreams
the 1000 of streams
i dream of every season
just to bring you
to finally move

move onto better things
it's the reason i'm insane
for you to see
that you belong to me

but until that reality hits
it's the reason i must miss
you next to me
it just might have to be

normal hours

june 4 2022 12:18pm

it was the way that you looked at me
the intoxicating eye contact that pulled me over
it was like i've been waiting my whole life for this
i met myself at the doorstep to your soul
and that's who i love most
your special quirks that are also mine
and the way you challenge me
and want me to grow in ways i believe i can not
but you're there
undenying support
endless conversations
it's like our souls were ripped away
and took lifetimes to find each other back
the birds sing in our glory
of love and whispers
from the smell of your touch
to the kiss of your sanction
i could not stop thinking about you
after we met
the thought of your soul kept me up all night
tossing and turning
until we could meet again
the thought of your eye contact
would make my heart quiver
you allow me to be myself
on my behalf
there is no trying
no denying
but to be myself
and that's what i love most

june 4 2022 12:18pm

i met my soul at your doorstep
completely needs be
my heart quivers
from the intoxicating look you gave me
the experience i've been searching for
became mystical

you make me feel worthy
when i am not
i do better be better
for me
but it's way more worth it
to do it for you

the artist in me
sees the artist in you
the creative
the luxurious
of all things holy
exist in our hearts

i saw the signs
from weeks before meeting
so when i gazed you
it was destiny
who met me on my doorstep

the birds in a pair
the penguins at my footsteps
the vibrating of my heart
was longing for you
the feeling i yearned for
the longing for my soul
was met at your doorstep

june 25 2022 8:21pm

to my future lover
i am a powerful being
i bring no man with me
unless he is the one

you must hold my power
with gentle and grace
because with a brush of a dusting
comes a whole wind storm

i have a big personality
my words are power
but my arms are a sanctuary
where you are so welcome

i am a sovereign being
as gentle as grace
your gift is my presence
may you never forget

you must love adventures
and also a challenge
my love is a thousand rose petals
times a billion

my touch is soft
such subtle and sweet
but my power is in my heart
that vibrates freely

i need my alone time
to rest and recharge
only to be met
by your love, in my arms

july 22 2022 8:49pm

bathed in grace
i am floating in space
caved in the way you're captivated by the stars that shine above you
caved in the way you inspire me to love

                                                bathed in grace
                                           i could say your name
                                          twice before you left
                                          but never will forget
                                         the last kiss you laid
                                     upon my maiden face
                                      the lace i was wearing
                                 the truth you were daring
                       the way your eyes glared at mine
                                       the stars they shine
                                     for your loving grace
                                 bathed in the moon light
                                           summer nights

october 18 2022 8:59am

i know more than i allow myself to feel
for the fear of being wrong
mistaken
but what is life
if the risk is not taken
it's all just an experience
just an experience
feel it

october 29 2022 8:39am

you are my everything
my every waking thought
day dream
how are you not mine
how am i so lucky
to be smitten by you
all the fucking time
you're on my mind
24.7
it's a gift truly
you in my life
it's like summer
all the fucking time

how did i get so lucky

november 4 2022 7:19pm

i have conversations with you in my head
while i'm laying in bed
thinking about the last time we spoke
and the next time we'll speak
thinking about you
and me
it's an endless cycle
on repeat
you drown my thoughts
my every waking breath
to be next to you
lying in this bed

the dream
the wish
the unspoken kiss
that lingers in my head
waiting for you
pretty boy

november 4 2022 7:31pm

you're on my mind
it's like columbine
taking over my thoughts
with no one to save me
but you
even though
you're the one
holding the gun

november 4 2022 7:38pm

you my friend
are the reason
why stars exist

something to look at
something to gaze
they're always there
to take your breath away

like the stars they shine
you're on my mind
24.7

i've only met you twice
but in my mind
we've known each other
a thousand lifetimes

your breath is my every wish
every waking thought is you
how could you be so perfect
you were designed for me

am i taking over your mind?
like you've intruded mine
it's causing agony
of my other thoughts
there are none
you are my everything

am i crazy?
oh yes.
but you like that.
and i like that, too.

november 4 2022 7:38pm

are you mad boy?
are you unshakingly, inhabitedly mad boy?
so mad
that you make up words
to explain
how fucking mad you are

your mind is dark
and i like to go there
it complements
my lightness

the polarity
masculine
feminine
it is so divine
you complement me
like fine wine
that i don't drink

it's like
i never wanted to be this person
until i met you
and i love this person
when i met you

you're my favorite escape
lullaby
i can't wait to show you these poems

you thought you were the mad one?
boy.

my boy.

november 5 2022 3:40pm

when will you realize
that all the lies
you tell yourself
are the reason
you're still the same

person to blame
with every storm
that crosses your brain
you're the reason i'm insane

you're the reason i'm insane
the reason i'm insane
you're the reason i'm insane

but i can't stop
your smell is addicting
the sweet adolescence
i see in your protection
your protection from the shadows
that you glue to me

i'm stuck on your behalf
the love you'll never have
of mine
because i'm the queen
of self sabotage
oh my when will i survive

the turmoil it takes
to make me miss you
the turmoil i make
that hesitates to kiss you

november 5 2022 3:40pm

oh when will i realize
that you were mine
with out a doubt
my sweet sunshine

the reluctant ghost
that refuses me the most
to kiss you

the chance i'll never get again

the chance is lost to see you
because you've moved on
my adolescence surprise
my sweet adolescence boy

my sweet adolescence boy
my sweet adolescence boy

you feel sane to my brain
but you're the reason i'm insane
insane for you
your love is such a mystery
oh please repeat the history
the destiny of our love
i feel it in my bones
my skin
my knees are weak for you and only you
boy you're a blessing
the blessing
i've been waiting for
how could i have missed all the signs
my twin flame you'll be all mine
my sweet surprise

my adolescence boy

november 5 2022 3:40pm

our love is immortal
our souls eternal
i love that you love darkness
i am the light that compliments you
that feeds your needs
you're all i please
the pleasure is truly mine
my sweet surprise
adolescence boy

i spit fire when i think of you
thinking all these thoughts
that run my mind
oh boy but you're mine
only in my head
where are you now
i miss you so
are you thinking about me too
oh sweet surprise

you'll be mine
my sweet adolescence boy

500 miles away
oh boy
i never saw the day
coming to the end is near
the wait is clear
oh my sweet surprise
my adolescence boy

november 5 2022 3:40pm

the time is near
where i shed the tears
of all the times i cried
before i knew
you'd be mine
by my side
all the time
my sweet surprise
our love is why
my soul's alive
you're the reason i survived
all this time
my sweet surprise
my adolescence boy

i can't believe my own eyes
that you're all it takes to make me realize
that god is right
he's always on time
with the love he promised me in my own dream time
that's right
you were mine all along
this whole time
i just had to wait

november 6 2022 7:01pm

my heart is yours
when will it ever not be

destined for you
my heart burns

intoxicated by your being
entirely over whelmed

drowning in your presence
unsecured devotion

yearning
wishing
feeling
sadness

where is your mind
when you think of me

when will be the day
i see you again

please don't be here just for my art

be here forever in my heart

november 7 2022 7:21am

i dreamed you
i wished for your existence

i created you in my heart
flustered by the insanity
that you don't want me

or it makes it seem

why must i be so aggressive
it's the love i know i deserve
grasping by the thought of
what if i'm not good enough

what if it's too good for me

where does unworthiness come from

is it the saint tropez dream?

why are you in my life
you started as a dream
a wish
a ponder
a waking thought

now you walk right in front of me

past me

through the doors of eternal
our souls
our bodies
they're immortal

november 7 2022 7:21am

i knew you in a past life
i had to
you're way too familiar

and now you're walking past me
in this lifetime

the flowers i grip on so hardly to
are suffocating
just like the worthiness
the love i have for myself
where did it go?

are you more than just a dream?
i'm smitten
intoxicated by your presence
it keeps my every waking thought alive
you consume my mind
it hurts like hell

to know i have no other thoughts
my dreams are desires
for you

do you think of me too?
day and night
like i do of you?

i miss you
how could i
we only met once
but many lifetimes before
we spent more time together
more time adored

november 7 2022 7:21am

fantasized by your hypnotizing lies
you do tell me
or so i think

why do i doubt myself
the ability to be loved
it seems so hard for me to believe
where does that come from
is it from the past
or inside of me?

the outcome of survival
is to cause fear in our head
because it never has to hurt us
if we decide to never rally

but what if it does
what if you take the risk
free falling
no expectations

are you telling me not to day dream?
how could you
tell that
to a dreamer

letting go of expectations
in this 3d world
let the 5d rally
my energy
my vibration
let it be happy
high vibration
let's keep high vibration

november 7 2022 7:21am

love
safety
stability
fearlessness
consciousness

new adventures
new desires
new kisses
new admirers

endless love
eternal beings
internal desires
external admires

i believe i love you
because i love myself
and myself created you

you're perfect
physically
but mentally
i don't know you
i'd like to think i do
i'll take the risk
in knowing you

in finding out who you are
let me be the feminine
show me your masculine
surrender to your willingness
take me for a wild ride
one i'll surely never forget

november 7 2022 7:29am

you're my sweetest desires on paper
in human flesh

november 7 2022 7:33am

do you hear me when i write of you
i know you're thinking of me too
of the last time we spoke
for that one time you wrote
my name in your phone

who am i in your mind?
i'm so curious
in mine you're divine
everything to me
my deepest desires fulfilled

but to you
who am i?

november 9 2022 8:55am

i have a love for myself
it's like nothing else
he tells me how beautiful i am
even when i storm
out of the room
because i'm thinking
of how much i love you

it's scary
and exciting
and i love all of it
i'm gracious
and patient
with the process
because i know it will be worth it

in the end
i expend
my energy towards you
but really
it's for myself

because i love myself
as much as i love you

november 13 2022 1:24pm

what makes you think being dark is a bad thing?

november 15 2022 9:46pm

waiting for your appreciation
is the initiation i will never be apart of
it kills me inside
knowing that a part of me has died
waiting for you,

it's agony in the sunrise
another day goes by
where i don't hear from you
another sun fall
and it seems like
i had it all
and then gone
but unlike the sun
you don't rise again

was it me?
something i said
or something unspoken
i held back for you
because that's what i thought you wanted
but i guess i was wrong
it's not what i thought

i assumed you were interested
like the cloud on a rainy day
but unlike the storm
when you passed
you never came back

november 15 2022 9:46pm

you followed her
she followed you
but what about my dreams
where i see the two
the two of us
laughing
having the time of our lives
all two in love
and then comes the sunrise

the sunrise
the sunrise

just you and i
till the end of time
just until
another sunrise

                                        never let it end

november 19 2022 7:14pm

i want to tremble in your ecstasy
pickled by your essence
i hate that word
but it's the only way to describe
i want to be saturated in your presence
your love
infatuation by your touch
the never ending temptation to kiss you
the foreseen shaking of your finger tips
as they caress over my body that burns for you
the feelings you pulse through my heart when you're
not near
i feel you
i can hear you in my thoughts
the idea of you
makes me swept
my heart yearns for you
like a cosmic storm in my chest
our souls dancing in the ethers
lifetimes before
destine to meet again
on this new earth

november 19 2022 7:14pm

you crossed my path
when i was discovering mine
my truth
my earth's journey
my awakened soul
kindred spirit

how fond i am of your gaze
the last gaze
you gave me
in my dreams we talk
we touch
we have everyday lives
they live in my head
in the ethers of dream time

i love our connection
i love what we have
inside my head
but the anticipation of feeling it
on a physical realm
makes me quiver to the bone
the thought of finally feeling you
actually
truly
touching me
kissing me
the thought makes my whole body shiver
like fairies dusting my skin
the most intense feelings of love in my heart
open to receive
you

november 19 2022 7:14pm

do you think about me too?
aware of this journey?
do you feel my presence?
the love i send?
the energy that is present?
i love you.

i pray for the day
i see you next
in real time
dream time is where magic happens
where my memories are stored
i feel you there
on an energetic realm
but to feel you in real life
only time will tell

but if time doesn't exist
how about now?
do you feel that?

will you read my poems i made for you one day?
do i feel comfortable to show you?
what if you laugh.

because i always knew
from the moment i met you
you probably will think i'm crazy

                                            that's because i am

november 19 2022 7:14pm

you tell me you're dark
well baby
i am the dark goddess

what if the day never comes
i question that
i do…
because i'm scared
i'm making this all up

what if i am?

what if it is just a fairy tale.
how will i face the truth
i'd be a fool
ashamed

because what i thought i once wanted…
wanted nothing to do with me.

but better always came,
this or something better
you seem like better

it's so easy
you are there
right.
there.
i had you.
and then you ghosted.

you ghosted me.

november 19 2022 7:14pm

how dare you
i thought it was love
is it still there?
what do you think of me?

am i just a young girl
 a stranger
that you once knew

the promises you made
are you running from them?

you're on your journey.
and that's okay

because i'm on mine too

but i know for me
i will focus on me
and hopefully you will come
i love you,
but that's because i love me

that sounds fucking crazy to me
am i crazy to write that?
love?
what is it that i love?

i love the idea of you
of you feeling me
touching me
it's all physical
i love the physicality of it

november 19 2022 7:14pm

i don't even know you
i feel like i do
in my head
i've made up a story
about you
i feel like i know you
in my head

i said i love you.
i said i love you
am i crazy?

i thought you were the one
thought?
think?
what am i saying?

who am i
i'm questioning
i'm getting too logical.

it's the logic
the logic is killing me
questioning my feelings

i've gone too deep

i am crazy
like you called me

crazy girl

i will forever cherish that

november 19 2022 7:14pm

you recognized me for my true self

you made me feel seen
feel heard

i was acknowledged for who i really am

crazy

crazy artistic
talented
in love

please come to me
in a matter of time
before i let you go

but what if i let you go
and you come to me

i have laundry to do

i must now focus on me

okay?

november 20 2022 9:02am

i dreamt of you last night
you're the memory that shapes me
though i can't remember the dream
i know you were there
gazing into my eyes
you touched my soul
like no one else
has done before

last night broke the barrier
i said i love you
with your name attached
it hit different
it made me question my insanity
but i know you love my insanity
so maybe that was the answer i needed
the reassurance
that i'm doing something right in this world

you broke the barrier for me
i've become obsessive
compulsive
quick
but it all is for love
to feel a sense of pleasure
outside of myself

i crave pleasure
outside of myself

to seek that i need to create pleasure inside of myself
for you to hear me
in the ethers and beyond

november 20 2022 9:02am

thank you for the magic you've given me
even if you don't know it yet

                                        …until we meet again

november 20 2022 9:44pm

strangers
until we're not

november 19 2022 10:12pm

the anticipation for you to notice me

november 21 2022 7:43am

i dreamt of you last night
so i slept a little longer

am i forcing these dreams?
or are you really coming to visit me?

am i just a stranger to you?
we all start out as strangers

what did you want from me
that now you call me a stranger

how could you push me away
so easily

our connection
it was so good

was it too good?
too real for you?

you are dark
and you showed me darkness

but i love the dark
so you have me chasing you

you're the runner
i'm the chaser

the twin flame reunion
i've been anticipating for

november 21 2022 7:43am

the initiation
it was you all along

spirit showed me the signs
i was mistaken for lost souls

you are my twin flame journey
is this just a trauma bond?

you showed me lessons
i could have never seen myself

i thank you for that
i honor that

i have compassion for you
that you're on your twin flame journey too

may you find grace
was i too real for you?

was it when i looked you in the eye and i saw your soul
you accused me of psychoanalyzing

how did you know?
you would only know, if you could feel me.

i can feel you in my bones
deep in my core

can you feel me too?
our souls connect on different realms

november 21 2022 7:43am

the hesitations to text you
i have never

did you have hesitations texting me?

i know you saved those for me
or did you…

am i assuming the magic you created for me?

is this all in my head
no

my mind says no
my heart? it wants you more

i'm sad i told people about you.
i'm actually mad

you were special. and now i share this journey with others.

they ask questions
i explain
but they don't get it
they don't get it like i do

do you get it like i do?

november 26 2022 6:04pm

i'm not sure if you're my forever

but you showed me what forever looks like

november 23 2022 12:52pm

my poems to you have come to a rest
i feel safe once again in your presence
the void seems to be filled
with comfort
security

i was in pain
fear
scared
i did something wrong

i surrender
i set the ties loose

and you came back
what a learning lesson

trust
trust
trust

release the ties
the hard grip

you came back

and i'm flattered

smitten perhaps

…see you tomorrow

november 27 2022 8:19pm

where do you go when i fall asleep
where i'm dreaming of you lying next to me

it sombers my heart
but who made being dark a bad thing

i burn so hard for you
it's been months since i've felt normal
but i guess normal, was broken

you made me feel complete
you make me feel complete

i want to be with you. all the time
it hurts to know, i am not

do you want to be with me too?

i make art for you.
it's all for you.
it's like my life, i'm doing it for you

where is this coming from?
the delusion

it seems a delusion

my obsession
i'm scared to admit
even to myself

november 27 2022 8:19pm

it's all so real
unworldly
it's actually not even real
it's the fantasy i've always dreamed of

you were there when i discovered myself

the journey i am on
you are there
standing next to me
you were the catalyst

i did it all for you
yes for me
but you were the game changer

and i want to share with you
all the amazing things i've experienced
all my stories

i want to hear from you

but you've been distant
are you scared?

oh boy. i'm scared too

it's all so scary

being open, vulnerable

but we can be scared together

december 1 2022 1:43pm

waiting for you to walk in is like waiting for the past
to arrive

you make me hate me
even when you're not there
to remind me
i'm no good
and you want nothing to do with me
as you should

i gave you the power
the first time we met
and it seems to me
you ran away with grace

december 1 2022 9:14pm

waiting for you
is like waiting for flowers to bloom
in a garden that has no sunlight

december 2 2022 7:53pm

thank you god
for the chalice i carry
of hope and grace
and the divine i face
serves me on the daily
for the chalice i carry
reminds me of you

for the chalice i carry
holds your heart

december 2 2022 7:53pm

you hold the chalice of my heart
in the ecstasy of your presence
you allow my soul to come alive
in the unfolding of your divine masculine
my heart yearns for you in a thousand times
across the pond i see your gaze
it brings me to my knees
i submit to the unwavering faith of your true nature
the ability to release under your control
drives me through a portal of liberation
profoundly yours beyond death
many deaths we've encountered
experienced
for played
but nothing like the death of our ego
when we collided
you're my soul's twin
no separation
we are one
and i've waited many lifetimes
to experience a reunion like this
12.2.2022

december 13 2022 11:03pm

i miss when you use to ask when i'll be gone
or how i'm doing
i miss how you called me crazy
crazy girl
maybe i was just
too crazy for you
you asked
and i showed you

december 17 2022 3:24pm

i use to fall for you
soul i have not met before
the burden
the kiss
of death to us hollow
the hollowing of our hearts
the incredible gift of your long lasting love
lust
it was only ever lust

the tension i bare when i'm near you
the quivering of my soul's thirst
quenched by the aroma of your skin
my bones shake bare for you up against me
the dopamine rush of just the thought
of you
that is not lust my friend
that is love
sweet decadent desire
feed my soul its needs
and i will never let a day pass by
where you're not my ecstasy

my soul rush
from your touch
the anxious thoughts that consume me
when you're not around
the ever lasting dopamine from
the taste
of you
the rapture of your burdens
do you rage for me
the skill it takes to ignore you
absolutely mad hattering

december 17 2022 6:36pm

sometimes the knots we carry are meant to stay to
attract the people we need most

december 18 2022 5:41pm

the ability to speak
your native tongue
has me weak at the knees
the expansiveness won

won my heart in the kingdom
of seldom grey
the ability to speak
as your woman slave

i bow on my knees
for your sovereignty
the grace
the music
the exotic touch
your masculine taste

until the day comes
where i can feel you physically
you're only in my thoughts
everyday
24.7
until i'm blue in the face

i love what we have
inside my head
i pray for the day to come
to wake up next to you
in your own bed

december 18 2022 5:41pm

i dream of us together
laughing, housing
being soulmates
twin flames
in 3d reality

do you believe in the matrix
as i sure do
i believe in true love
where is your trust
where is your burn
i burn for you

december 17 2022 9:05pm

blinded by
the love i sought out externally
was the love i found for myself
mirrored by
my twin flame

december 17 2022 9:05pm

the waking angsts
of your anxiety
pulses through my sobering skin
as your anti tongue speaks

i bow on my knees
for your sovereignty
the ability to speak
your native tongue
has me weak at the knees

my renaissance man
did i meet you there
where our love was flourished
and left the only language i ever knew

december 22 2022 5:12pm

my renaissance man
did i meet you there
where our love was flourished
and left

you took my heart
and stabbed it into pieces
you threw my art in the fire
my soul's desires
and now
i have unfinished business
i seek in this lifetime

to share my heart
and collect all the pieces of myself
i once forgot
for retaliation
that i crave so deep
in my soul's time

and to rebuild the only language i ever knew

love

xx,

december 22 2022 5:12pm

my heart of course
speaks a thousand languages
besides the one
you reside in

december 22 2022 5:12pm

when will you show me the sovereignty of your love
that i crave so deeply
the deep desire to feel
you inside of me
the incredible opportunity
to feel my past
the familiarity of your sound
your eyes
your family crest
it's here
it's now
it's happening soon
i am so grateful
so thankful
you had me swoon
over your style
over your face
everything about you
i love
with exotic taste
my lasting impression
was my first desire
to love you to pieces
the ultimate fire
the twin flame bond
speaks so loudly
i didn't guess it for a second
a moment
a lifetime
i want you
so badly

xo - yours so truly

december 22 2022 4:24pm

it was the ecstasy of your voice
that had me smitten
from the day we first met
to the words that were written

upon meeting you
i journaled and day dreamed
about the moment
i would be freed

from the longing wish
of feeling your touch
from the unspoken man
my true love's crush

december 25 2022 7:27am

you kissed me in my dream last night
i was talking nonsense
you grabbed me by the waist
and shut me up
and just like that
i was falling

i couldn't sleep
but some how
you showed up in my dreams
you grabbed me by the waist
and kissed me
and ever since then
i've been falling

you grabbed me by the waist last night
you kissed me hard and softly
whispered in my ear
& it wasn't till then
i began to fall
back asleep

you kissed me in my dream last night
and i've never wanted so bad
to fall back asleep
even though
my dreams use to haunt me
until you showed up

i use to be afraid of sleep
until you kissed me in my dream last night
and ever since then
i've been falling

december 28 2022 11:08am

you come at me with your daggers
but i take them and dance

january 2 2023 2:19pm

2022
is when i met you
the gust in the wind
your breath on my skin
the ultimate affair
take me there

                                              take me there
                               until we're burly bare
                         surrender to the madness
                                  of our soft sins
                              that no other human
                           would ever understand
                             but it doesn't matter
                                 because we do
                                you're my 2022

2022
is when i met you
on the doorstep of my summer days
you took my heart away with you when you left
and then you came back
it was magic

january 3 2023 9:07pm

take me to oblivion with your words
allow me to unravel in your presence
touch my skin until i'm raw in the flesh
the sovereign kiss upon my lips
brings me feeling that not even ecstasy could

the soul presence of your flame
the double letters in your name
allows me comfort where no forest could claim
true nature
in its name
you're my journey
my earth plane

match my soul
till death do us

january 5 2023 3:08pm

when i met you, i changed
into the version of myself
i never thought was imaginable
i day dreamed about her
the stories she will tell
the way she will feel
her sacred style
i've never felt that kind of love in my life before
you activated something inside of me i can't explain
but it was the best damn drug i've ever taken

january 5 2023 8:18am

i am riding the void into oblivion
where the depths of our soul will anguish
collapse as one
surrender to oneself
the anguish of our sorrows
will soon be banished
after the surrender
comes the union
the union of love
sanction unity oneness

i write about you at 2am
you carry me back to sleep
with your words so deep
in my brain
you drive me insane
until i can not sleep no more
nights awake
i cry i escape
the soul burning for you
to devour me with your words
until we meet again
my soul flame

i feel so complete with this
there is absolutely no doubt
no belief in my head
that could tell me any different
there is not even a cell in my body
that doubts our love
and if you call me crazy
i want nothing more
than to be clinically insane
in love with you,

january 5 2023 8:18am

i want you to show me all the music
you think i'll love
not because you love it too
but because you love me enough
to pick the songs you know i'll like

january 5 2023 8:39pm

i have never been so sure in my life
that you are my forever
from the depths of my bones
to every cell
you are the one

january 9 2023 4:11pm

i want to hear the inside of your heart
all the trials
you put yourself through
before i met you

                                      i dreamt you made me a playlist
                                  and as little as that seems to be
                                          it's all i ever wanted

to hear the insides of your heart

january 9 2023 4:11pm

i'm still running from your heart
that you left on my doorstep
on that summer afternoon
when i first met you

and from that moment on
you haven't left my mind
you were fireworks in my heart
like the 4th of july

january 9 2023 4:11pm

you left foot prints on that doorstep
and ever yet

                                        i felt fireworks in my heart

january 9 2023 5:17pm

you left tattoos on my heart
with words you never said
the feelings i wish you meant
covered me in dread
knowing you'll never
feel the same

january 12 2023 1:59pm

not much makes sense
no logic
could ever call it
what it is
you hold inside of me
your brain
must be insane
to not see the glory
i have for you
i day dream
i plead
for you on your knees
begging me
to unlock the key
because after all
you're my velvet wall

crushed by the thought
the instance
the coincidence
it was to meet you
when nothing went astray
you were there
on that summer day
paralysis
beyond this mess
co create
deliberate
the absolute thought of you
has me on my knees
begging please
unlock the key
because after all
you're my velvet wall

january 12 2023 1:59pm

the ocean doesn't make sense
the waves
create
things we don't anticipate
the moon
gathers thoughts
that my words will never speak
because when i think of you
down on one knee
it all makes sense
no consequence
there's no ring involved
because at the end of it all
you gave me the key
to your velvet wall

i've cut ties with you
what is there to lose
no more playing small
when you wish to have it all
the glory
the peace
in lying next to you
with you all over me

i fantasize
paralyzed
by the thought of you
on your knees
begging me
to taste you
after all
you're my velvet wall

january 12 2023 1:59pm

i don't want the key to your heart
it's the art i crave
i want the soul shattering
worlds collapsing
absolute travesty
of a fucked up sinner
man that you are

simply for the art of it

january 18 2023 1:22pm

waiting for your reply
on the text i never sent
because i'm too scared
you won't be there

you'll think of me
in someone else's dream
because i constantly think
you're too good for me

but the reason i'm insane
is for us to blame
we're the perfect pair
and i don't care
how long it takes

you're my mistake

december 30 2023 10:31am

the sun on your face
will never be the same again
because the stars when they shine
they tend to remind
that you were just false hope
and the rain just won't stop
in the everdeen drop
of faith i held for you
but you never really knew
because every time it hit
it was always such a miss
opportunity for the truth
it was all i could do
at the time
but now time's passed
and you're still not mine
you're gone
i realized i was wrong
for the stars they don't shine
a million reasons why

i'm lost

january 18 2023 1:22pm

watching the clouds migrate
while mercury retrogrades
wishing for you to hold space
for me to unravel

january 19 2023 8:38am

it was the ocean air
that took me there
to a place of magic
and make believe
from the salty earth
to the sandy sea
it wasn't until then
when i realized
that it was always you
on my mind
ocean air
take me there

it was the shiver of the earth
that left you under my skin
from the blood shot eyes
to the porcelain skin
you are everything i imagined
but better and more
suitable for love on my arms
waiting at the door

those doorstep eyes
they were magnetized
from your wide brimmed hat
on that welcome mat
i felt so shy
smitten as day
your calm and collected
kept me at bay

january 19 2023 8:38am

i gave you for the summer days
spent in the colorado hay
i'll let you go
but i didn't even know
you'd walk back into my life
those moon sent eyes
now they're,
forever mine

the twin flame curse
oh, it might be the worst
in the best way possible
exactly no cause of all
the heartbreak yearning
the painful separation
all those hard earning task
it was all in operation
to bring us together
to live a perfect forever
it took the pain
from that summer day
to say, this is who i am
this is who we are
oh, it's meant to be
but i must leave you a far
so you can grow
evolve
become the best you
the best know it all
and until we're both ready
the perfect match
separated at first
before ever last

january 19 2023 7:52am

held by your neck
every last breath
i spent
on you

it was the long winter nights
that left me a fright
that you'd never reach out
oh i was so afraid

it wasn't until
the very next day
when i untied the strings
you were right next to me

to cut the cords
the loose ends set free
you were then
lying next to me

i imagined the day
oh the very next day
you'd never forget
you'd always stay

but until i release you
i will never please you
because a flower will suffocate
if you don't release to fate

january 21 2023 11:55am

the brilliance is in the wound
the heart break for the matter
it's the sound of your voice
that makes my heart
pitter patter

the depths of your soul
no one can see
it's the brilliance in the beauty
of you right next to me

the darkness of your ally
that causes me to choke
the witness in the valley
of your pretty natured cloak

cloak of darkness
rest over me easy
because with out you
i can hardly breath

the missing piece
in my soul's destiny
but you're not awake
puts the dagger
through the stake

january 21 2023 7:53pm

current standards
seem imminent
it's the way you grace
forever infinite

to run to scream to ache
until you're next to me
oh what it feels

january 21 2023 8:53pm

i want to be
immersed in your darkness
saturated by your light
absorb your every thought
until our universe collides

immersed in your darkness
darkened by the sea of light
lit by the ocean
on a dark winter's night

released by the sea
right here next to me
drifted away
through the crippling breeze

released by your darkness
your deepest desires
shadowed by the light
of your heart's burning fire

it's you i see
all over me
that drives me back
to the dark winter sea

released by your darkness
your deepest desires
shadowed by fate
the blood sunken fire

january 21 2023 8:53pm

released by your darkness
relieved by the pain
the sea produces more
nothing feels the same

released by your darkness
the fiery fate
the tumbling goddess
of my soul sinking faith

released by your darkness

released by your darkness

it's you i craaave
it's you i crave

january 21 2023 9:04pm

as i sit in silence
upon the gaze
of your blood shot eyes
it's you that i've missed

to be with you now
was my last dying wish
to remember the touch the escape
of our past life's kiss

the depths of our soul
shake up lifetimes below
it's you that i've missed
from a couple centuries ago

it feels like forevers ago
where you were last next to me

                                          why did it take so long

january 21 2023 9:04pm

the depths of our soul
shake up lifetimes below
where you were last next to me
true loves meant to be

and it feels like forever
my toxic endeavor
that my last dying wish
was our past life's kiss

to be with you now
in this lifetime with me
reminds me of the broken heartache
that keeps happening

because the irony is
the truth to be
it was never true love
rather a karmic destiny

january 21 2023 9:04pm

come at me with a playlist
and i'll be yours forever
show me the song of your soul
that will tie us together

to my toxic endeavor
with all the right pleasure
the cause and the kiss
it's forever, i miss

to be next to you now
not just lifetimes ago
i want i crave i need to hear
the sound of your soul

the lingering kiss
that you have yet to share
on my sweet smitten lips
that are left an unwilling bare

to be with you now
to feel that daggering kiss
the constant fury
of our lifetime's wish

to call it crazy
that is an honor to be
because if i know one thing
it's that crazy
               loves
                         crazy

january 22 2023 9:18am

thank you god
for the love that leaves me quivering
for every day's a new adventure
the sweet sound
of our souls together

happiness

january 23 2023 8:34pm

wanting to hide again
bury under the pain
this healing journey
it's never the same

the pain it takes
to make the rain stop
in the same way
causes it to stay

you can't control a storm
no matter how hard you try
because mother nature
takes no misery light

she sheds her wisdoms
she sheds her ways
but she does it
so nothing stays the same

and in that way
we have seasons and falls
because when the rain stops
that's when beauty calls

it's the same way
nature makes its season
even if
we have no reason

to stay the same
is a selfish way
to cause a catalyst
in your stubbornness

january 23 2023 8:34pm

because if we grow from nothing
nothing changes
it's the way god intended it
we grow in phases

the pain the fury
of the hard lessons
it's life itself
it's full of blessings

if we choose to view it
from a catalyst point
that the shifts and changes
are nothing but, amazing

are nothing but,
amazing

because we grow
we grow in phases

that's the way
nature changes.

january 24 2023 6:59am

the burn
the burn it purifies
it purifies and shakes
shakes me back to you

the blood
the blood it seeps
it purifies and bleeds
bleeds me back to you

this city burns
my heart up in flames
feelings are not the same
it's all from you

the fury aches
the pain irritates
the ground it shakes
shakes me back to you

this burning feels
it feels so real
it burns and breaks
my heart won't hesitate
me back to you

the fury feels at stake
the query imitates
my heart feels no sane
it's all because of you

                                        the journey back to you

january 24 2023 6:59am

the burning field desire
i watch it burn in fire
the ground it levitates
my heart devastates
all from you

i was so insane
to think you so innate
you feel internalized
my heart, was full of lies

tied to your chain
wrapped around my own brain
you were my ecstasy
a burning part of me

but it never materialized
i fed all the lies
it was a suffocate
a love struck so detained

i feel so much pain
your ground doesn't shake
i feel paralyzed
from all the lies
i tell myself
about you

the journey back to you

january 24 2023 6:59am

a love struck so inveined
a remedy in my brain
but the feeling lies
in the unmaterialized

the feelings so mundane
without you in my day
a missing piece inside
a soul without a life

the feelings come at night
when i'm sitting in star light
i look up to watch the day
as it fades away

intrigued by the way
you make me feel insane
i want you
my twin flame

you're ecstasy in my day
the way you make me feel sustained
with your moon lit eyes
that's where the love struck lies

the feelings have no blame
on the days i feel this way
because these moon lit eyes
i can't help but fantasize

the way you say my name
it fuels me full of fame
your true nature imitates
my soul for heaven sake

january 24 2023 6:59am

our story has no name
you're perfect just the way
i left you at heavens gate
you're my twin flame

because love is disguised
within these 3d lies
but you know it's sane
the way it makes you feel,

i miss you. i do. my soul - it burns for you. it's the
journey that led me here. it's where i last felt whole.
it hurts when you're not around. i ache and i sore. i
knock on heaven's door. asking when you'll be
around again. but no answer. it's the unknown that
hurts. it's the feeling at worse. your mind is so insane.
it's perfect in every way. it's the remedy for my brain.
other feelings - so mundane. i want you for heaven's
sake. what's stopping you in the way? am i being
loud enough? my heart, she must be so quiet. roaring
on the inside of the gold plated chest i built for your
love to bury.

our love was like the renaissance as i last remember.
artistic, poetic, kinesthetic. everything about it was
true and prophetic.

but just like the renaissance, things have to crumble
and break. it sounds so cliché, but without you in my
day, the feelings are at stake. my heart quivers and
shakes. until you feel the pain, nothing will stay the
same. without you and your name. calling me,

your twin flame.

january 24 2023 10:29am

it hurts so deeply
when you are not near
i send it with my heart
are you able to hear?

i don't have the words
that are willing to speak
all the missing letters
 on this dear love streak

january 24 2023 10:44am

our banter is poetry

january 24 2023 11:03am

it was the way that you spoke to me
in your dark natured tongue
the sound of your voice
you had my heart strings strung

you're life's greatest element
that stepped into my life
the unspoken letters
i continue to write

i day dream about
the day we first met
it was love at first sight
you had my heart swept

to be with you now
the thought makes me quiver and shake
the feeling in my heart
it pains me to say…

i'm not sure if i'm right
from all the dark, sleepless nights
i stay up thinking of you
and if our love will ever bloom —

january 24 2023 10:00pm

my ultimate desire
comes with this grace
to light my soul on fire
and let it burn at the stake

must have been heaven's mistake
to put your blood in my veins
you were my darkest desire
that lit my heart on fire

the music you call home
causes my love to grow
it persuades me to change
in all the right ways

for the story of fate
to your blood written name
it's the journey at stake
that's the love of a twin flame

twin flame
do you hear me?
hear me calling
for the love of god
i've been falling
for your blood sunken eyes
you're like heaven disguised
to journey with you now
is like a god vetted vow
my heart burns for you
the silence causes unknown
but it's the twin flame journey
that causes my love to grow

january 24 2023 10:00pm

with you in my veins
love had no cost

only blood on the cross

january 24 2023 3:23pm

the happiest i've ever been
is swimming in the ocean
but with you on my mind
it feels like summer all the time

january 25 2023 2:52pm

i was blinded by your love
deprived from your ecstasy
was it love at first sight
or you just sitting next to me

the thought of you now
makes me cringe
but maybe that's just
all apart of it

the journey of twins
set from a flame
since the day that i met you
i only have our soul to blame

for feeling this angst
from creating this art
shot from the arrow
straight through my heart

it's you that i've longed for
my entire life's path
but this distance is agony…
waiting for our love to clash

xx

january 27 2023 9:30am

no need to explain
in fact
i'm sick, bed ridden
of trying to put logic
to this pain

this painful crutch
that's causing me to cry
it's the deep feeling in my lungs
it's a way
of wanting to die

but at the exact very same time
this feeling i sigh
is the exact same feeling
i've never felt more alive

to hear your name
across a room full of whispers
ripples my skirt
through a thousand doors

faster than a hummingbird's heart
you were the arrow
that shot
straight through my heart

january 29 2023 8:50am

pretty pretty pretty
take a chance on me
dwindling
down on your knees
hustling
there's no need
because i got you
taking care of your needs

honey honey honey
take a chance on me
standing
at the shore of your feet
because i got you
you're all that i need

january 29 2023 10:33am

it's the everdeen whispers
that causes our love to simmer
in the heart of summer days
it's you i want to lay

lay down your love
spread out your pieces
you're killing me softly
in the bed that creases

ever so sweetly
down to the touch
it's the feeling of sovereignty
that's causing me to bluff

because without you
i'm not sure who i'd be
the feeling inside
it's so meant to be

january 29 2023 10:41am

waking up
sweat drenched clothes
feelings
being exposed
wishing we'd never met
laying in this blood drenched sweat

the feeling of agony
the feeling of bliss
where were all the feelings
the feelings i missed

i must of been wrong
about you in my mind
it was the feeling of dying
coming from inside

that left me wondering
about our blood bonded fate
but it must have been
a love drunk mistake

because these sweat drenched clothes
this empty bed
has left you
just in my head

this feeling inside
with you on my mind
drives me to pieces
of wanting to cry

january 29 2023 10:41am

to cry for our love
to seek out our sovereignty
but it's none of that you want
it's none of that you say to be

you're so cynical
the songs you send me
but what if that's
just love envy

envy that you feel
and i feel it too
i can express it
but that's not what you choose

because you're just a little boy
so dark to be
but what you don't know
is that i'm the dark goddess you seek

you just see the outside
the no feelings of depth
it's the empty room i wake up to
that leaves our love feeling dead

it's the feeling inside
of you on my mind
these blood drenched clothes
covered in tears of mine

i take off my hoodie
to feel the breeze on my back
of wanting you close
there's no holding back

january 29 2023 10:41am

if it's fate that i seek
for our love's in between
why must it be
so hard to please

this feeling inside
of you on my mind
but all that i'm left with
are these wet clothes of mine

the 2am love songs
they will always persist
as long as if
your presence is missed

for this feeling inside
that's not even mine
leaves my blood sunken tears
as the last real sign

that you were never meant for me
and it was just for the poetry

                                                    thank you
                                                    i love you
                                                      delete

january 29 2023 12:47pm

waking up with songs in my head
writing lyrics
about the words you last said
sovereignty
down on my knees
begging for you
to finish the melody

january 29 2023 12:50pm

words written
so smitten
about the times
our love's bitten
bitten by cupid's
arrow and key
to unlock
our true love's
fate to be

january 30 2023 11:48am

i felt your presence at 2am
you come to me in my sleep
only i'm not dreaming
i'm wide awake you see

i can't sleep anymore
without you next to me
you're all i ever think about

                                        simply just a day dream

january 31 2023 10:25am

as the selenite breaks
it reminds me of our fate
one soul
two dates
brought to earth
to separate
for our souls mission
to anticipate
so what this selenite means
is that
our divine union
is all what it's meant out to be

january 31 2023 12:13pm

as the selenite breaks
my soul begins to shake
knowing that
divine union
is at the stake

the stake of our love
the union's eternal
the shaking of the grave
of our separation's funeral

i feel it in my bones
our destiny being
true love at its finest
divine union to be

beauty had to break
for our love to be free

february 3 2023 7:44am

the parts of you
the parts of me
they're still inside us
secretly
wanting to
escape the seems
to reach a point
of sovereignty

the simplicity
to our destiny
is for one of us
to unlock the key

i gave you the key

                        and it seems

                                          you ran away with grace

february 5 2023 7:25pm

from the deaths of my health
to my highest self
you were the catalyst

the one who changed me
for the better
the one who held up a mirror
to my shadow endeavors

i changed in a way
that made you stay
and that wasn't even the best part

the best part was letting go
to the past ego
of who i thought i was

you came into my life
at the ultimate time
when the mastery of success
was searching for my best

i was use to loving you
from a far beyond place
that when you held up a mirror
it was my own face

faithful my darling
you won't be needing me
it's me needing you
it's the ultimate truth
you're right where i want you
and i'm almost there,

                                          please wait

february 9 2023 9:22am

i didn't want to be a crazy girl
but i've been losing my mind over you

february 13 2023 9:18am

the disrespect
of all the text
all the words
you left unsaid

in my mind
you were all the time
but it never hit me
that maybe

it was just a crutch
of this endless love
i had for myself
and nobody else

you were the catalyst
for my journey's mist
but that was it
it was all a miss —

                          missed opportunity
                                 for the truth
                it was never about loving you
                           but finding my

                                     bloom,

february 13 2023 10:33am

i'll never be able to tell
if that was cupid's doing
or the devil's spell
when the dagger hit
the arrow sent from hell

february 16 2023 10:31am

it was the ocean air
that took me there
to a place of magic
and make believe
from the salty sand
to the rippling sea
it was heaven on earth
or what i dreamed it to be

february 16 2023 3:17pm

i can feel your thoughts about me
or what i'd hope it would be
about the last time we spoke
or the number you wrote
on my hand that evening

and it's our past life
that keeps me up at night
blinded by day
the silence takes flight

i'm obsessed with your voice
the way that you speak
anything you say
sounds like music to me

the whistling waters
of the ocean breeze
reminds me of you
our fate's destiny

i dreamt about you
i cared about you
i wrote about you
i'm crazy about you

i can't believe you don't feel this
or maybe you do
what matters most
is that i met you

february 16 2023 3:17pm

at a time in my life
where i needed a sign
oh boy did i get the signs
you were my heaven surprise

i've channeled your angels
the ones who know me most
like a thief in the night
i'll be your ghost

who carries her voice
through the room that speaks
with my written sayings
and what i hoped this love
would be

but from all the sleepless nights
of wanting to be free
i realized
it was just a number you wrote
on my hand that evening

february 16 2023 3:28pm

to my love,
you always knew, even before we said i do. your passions fulfill me, to the brim of expansion. created by touch, expands in this mansion. in the house that we've built together, where our dreams come true. a second doesn't go by, when i'm not dreaming of you.

my love, you run so deep inside of me. your touch makes me quiver, the love that we simmer. your beauty excites me. to the point of exhaustion. exhausted by daylight, revived by your potion. the scent of your skin, nestled by fury. the way you channel the dark, ever so surely. i love that you're brave, that made me stay. your ever longing glory, will forever be the trademark in our story.

thank you for finding me. for searching the quest, it was the journey i've been craving and boy it was the best. your songs that we sing, our songs that you sing, will forever be the anthem of our soul. our one soul. twin flame journey.

you've showed me the way, the way to my own heart, just by being you, your dark foolish art. your brave silhouette crosses my mind, you drive me crazy, i'm so glad you're mine.

you make me feel amazing, even when i know i'm not. thank you for letting me be the man i needed to be before our love became 3d. thank you for being patient. thank you for never giving up.

you're my poetic queen. our poetic love. our souls are one.
                    it was the story of a life time.
                                         xx,

february 17 2023 2:07pm

freezing cold conditions
forces me to listen
to the things left unsaid
that are caught up in my head

it's cold as ice
in the middle of the night
that draws me to you
until day light

when i wake up missing
the text worth wishing
of things you'd say
the very next day

but the news of it all
it was the very best fall
now empty in my bed
because it was all
just in my head

february 19 2023 6:55pm

waiting for you to come home is like waiting for the
never ending storm
broken hearted
by the departed
of our last conversation
spent missing in bed
while i lay my head thinking of you
on that summer afternoon

incredibly easy
i wish it could be
but it's nothing but
dauntless days waiting for the storm to pass
and for you to miss me
like i miss you
on that summer afternoon

the poetry in my head
leaves me restless
it leaves my soul fed
with the idea of the reckless
insanity you brought to my mind
wishing you were with me all the time

but the reality is
truth come to be
that i miss you
more than you miss me

and that is why
our past lives
will remain in the summer time
where we first met
on that fated doorstep

february 22 2023 1:05pm

there's music in my heart for you
words you have yet to know
the whispers of my soul
our love forever grows

in the depths of my subconscious
in the patterns of my heart
it was true love at first sight
that created all this art

the magic lies in the unknown
the surroundings of my mind
to know that i'm your forever
and you're forever mine

february 24 2023 7:06pm

i am love sick
absolutely love sick
the feeling is madness

stuck in a daydream
the feelings come unclean
the thought of your ecstasy
it absolutely kills me
the feeling of sovereignty
is absolutely lost
in a day dream

i need to come clean
free of your ecstasy
i'm addicted
to the madness
of this love sick feeling

the feelings are so sure
that our love is so pure
it's causing me to feel this
this love sick madness

the feelings are so cool
cooler than the un new
feelings i feel for you
in this sickening world
you're the one who i adore
this love sick
love sick madness

i wrote about you all the time
the feelings
they're all mine

february 24 2023 7:06pm

the feelings are so cruel
i can't keep my cool
because i think about you all the time
wishing that you were mine
but the thought of you is so cruel

all these written letters
they just keep getting better
because of the timeline
of reaching you all the time

it's this 3d world
that keeps me so insane
but if i know one thing
our hearts
can channel from all the planes

so even when you're not around
i can still feel you in my town
because it's in my heart space
where i feel you on most days

you bring safety to my life
by thinking about you all the time
the feelings are better yet
all the ones that are left unsaid

you're all my thoughts
the feelings of being distraught
missing you all night
it's those feelings like all the time

february 24 2023 7:06pm

i know you'll walk me home tonight
because with out you i won't feel alright
you're always in my head
so my safety is never left unkept

oh boy, i can't wait for the day
for you to see my pain
the agony i experienced
with out you on my lips

because i have you right there

february 24 2023 7:24pm

i have conversations with you in my head
while i'm laying in this bed
thinking about the last time we spoke
and the next time we'll speak

you see
it's this journey between us two
it drives me crazy.
because even though it's the toughest battle
i'd ever wish upon myself
it's everything i asked for
and more

i prayed for a slow burn
and boy
you're a never ending fire
that flickers my every wish
my every soul desire

it's like you're in my cells
at all times of the day
i've been searching for you forever
and forever you will stay

xx

february 28 2023 6:04pm

the pictures of you in my head
undressed in my bed
is it just my imagination
or creative inspiration

you've been my every waking thought
like an unspoken day dream
and the next time we meet
will lace our legacy

you've taken over my life
it seems my every thought
to not have you present
leaves my body distraught

from the agony of the kiss
that was teased on my lips
and the last time we spoke
has my neck hung in ropes

until the next time we meet
i will be chasing false ecstasy
because you've only been in my thoughts
like the unspoken day dream

for the magic of new love
the dying of a wish
is the only reason
i still choose to live

                                      i wonder if it's the same for you

march 1 2023 11:27am

the taste of you
lingering on my lips
has my soul
at its finger tips

reaching for you
in every phase of the moon
truly brings
my heart in swoon

the planets align
in oh so divine
for our souls best favor
leaving our love to savor

savor in the wishes
of the unspoken kisses
left on our lips
at our last soul eclipse

march 1 2023 11:33am

the thought of you
brings me straight to the moon
draws me to outer space
the unspoken place

the place where i meet you
at every which crossing
it's heaven on earth
i feel our souls belonging

i go here when i need you
when i'm missing your touch
it's my favorite place
my heart can't get enough

march 1 2023 11:33am

come get your knife
where you last left its dagger
straight through my heart
left my soul
                    shattered

march 2 2023 9:05am

signed with blood
across my skin
it wasn't until
you walked in

when my heart stopped
the ceiling fell
into my lap
my heart could tell

that it was fate all along
who was singing this song
and every time
i press to rewind

march 2 2023 9:51am

grieving something you've never had
has to be the most painful way to grieve
because you never got to taste
what it felt to be

to be truly in love
just teased by smitten
straight through my heart
i was surely bitten

bitten by your crutch
your soul's ecstasy
how i crave the taste
of something that will never be

                                                    the love i wanted to give
                                                    had no where to go

march 2 2023 9:58am

back to my poetry
where seems the only place
where i can talk to you in spirit
and tease your heart's embrace

march 2 2023 10:16am

for the sadness grows
inside my heart's true divine
how i crave the taste
of your heart's electrify

electrified by hope
lightened by the day
reliving the scenery
i saw that day in may

our true love began
in the stars far beyond
the journey to connect us two
was in my chart all along

i wrote about you
before i knew it was true
that you were my other half
it was destiny through & through

and for my poetry,

belongs to you.

march 3 2023 12:56pm

maybe you're not around
and just in my head
what will it take
to tie our souls sacred thread

the thread straight from my heart
where it seems your only place to be
what if this matrix
won't allow us to see

to see our souls evolution
through lifetimes of trial
the windows of darkness
the shadows of denial

denial of hope
that our souls meant to be
together in this life time
unless it's false destiny,

march 3 2023 6:00pm

the visions of you
keep me alive
even though
i'd rather die

to not feel your touch
on a daily basis
kills me inside
it brings me in rages

but the fury of glory
i see at the end of the road
is worth all the torment
in this turmoil world

xx,

until our world's collide

march 4 2023 12:17pm

i am the blue butterfly
ready to spread her wings in love
been deep in my coven
channeling from above

wrapped around her own finger
are the winter days that seem to linger
in the midst of everything
she's ready to spread her wings

in the name of love
in the trial of mystery
wondering when
she will reunite with destiny

to complete her love
that was searched out to be
maybe he will come
this coming spring

march 4 2023 1:21pm

acting as if nothings wrong
bursting at the seams
only to be rebuilt as strong
like the butterflies i see

        reaching through these cocoon lit walls
        trying to break myself free
        grasping for something so damn small
        feels like dying inside of me

                i can't seem to find a reason to stay
                something please
                worth the pray
                because i miss you every waking day

though the journey to our forever song
might take forever
and forever long

        but it's the reason i believe
        the butterflies i see
        is the butterfly in me

march 4 2023 1:35pm

buried inside
are the visions of you
sought out by fate
in my soul's view

the view from the outside
the view from within
keeps my love
feeling like sin

because loving you
is like loving death
inevitable to happen,
unfortunate side effect

march 4 2023 9:23pm

reaching for something that i can't control
it leaves me so vulnerable
activated by a crutch
it sounds so hard to avoid this rut

i can't believe i'm saying this
but you're the reason i must dismiss
that everything was once fine
until you came, sweet valentine

the days were so light and free
but now are filled with misery
because the only reason i haven't quit
was the false hope love
of past season's wish

i dreamt of a saint valentine
oh man a man i could call mine
a forever soulmate forever crush
but now i'm leaning on a crutch

to keep you in my mind so dear
it's bottled up and caused by fear
because the thought of you enjoying me
it's the false hope love
the misery

i feel you all so vulnerable
it's like the pages i could never tell
of the love and sweet poetry
that i write about you constantly

march 4 2023 9:23pm

i wonder if i'll ever tell
you the reasons our love once fell
upon a wish
by satan's kiss
because this love feels like
a hell sent risk

it's like i can't ever tell
if you can even try to speelll
love with one E and another L
or if you just end up spelling hell

to be insane in this world today
is the only reason i must stay
because insane creates
and crazy prays
for the simple times of love struck days

because you can't be crazy
without a love sick story
and crazy
            loves
                      crazy.

march 4 2023 9:23pm

roses are red
violets are blue
it's the love struck feeling
i never knew

could be this rough
forever torment
the reason why
my heart's forever spent

spent out on love
washed from lust
it is a feeling
you can not trust

because this love sick feeling
has me seeing
all the reasons
you kept fleeing

waiting for you
across the door
is forever more
a forever bore

it's the reasons why
my heart feels petrified
my heart in pieces
i can't unsee it

broken hearted
love departed
no good started
from your soul rotten

march 6 2023 4:43pm

i call you late at night
when the sky is falling asleep
i can hear you behind my moon lit eyes
i wish it was you over me

but it's the noise inside the echos
echos of my heart
the eros of my soul
forever do us part

part the ways you miss me
because it's different than mine
i miss you because i want you
you miss me like the sky

the sky that's always there
you never have to look
it's forever in the background
always there, never shook

except when you're alone
when the stars are shining bright
you're dying to look up
but you realize you are blind

march 14 2023 7:13pm

it's raining inside my head now
for all the words you said how
you'd be the one to miss me
but i'm searching for the puzzle piece
of where you said when
and how this is all inside my head
and now it's raining

march 16 2023 12:01pm

i am waiting for you to come home
to the home inside my soul
that i created for you
on that first day in june
but you'll never know
and i'll never show
because i hold it inside
with you on my mind
and that's all where it will ever be

march 31 2023 10:00pm

i miss when you would text me
now you've got the best of me
no where to be found
my soul
in love bounds

relapsed on your darkness
forever a burden
mistaken by the chance
of the angels that swarmed in

repressed by your distance
saddened by mistake
because it was a love drunk coma
my heart stabbed at the stake

you stole my heart

i gave it away

it was a love drunk

love drunk mistake

and now i'm only left

with these poems of ours

that you'll never read

because you're distant,

                                                         so far.

march 31 2023 10:00pm

you lit my art on fire
i'm forever so grateful
which is why i'll be
forever so faithful

faithful to our journey
destined by design
because if it wasn't for you
for myself, i'd never find

i found my soul
i found my purpose
but it wasn't until you
it just wasn't until you

april 2 2023 11:38pm

gutted by your sirens
all the angel threads
kept me in sequence
of all the words you said

caressed by your fury
safe in your presence
it's only in the distance
i'm alone in silence

taken out by the angel of death
fueled by the passion of fame
fame of the hearts intertwined
but one can not be named

because you see
it's you
i seek
every cell within me
it's you
i speak,

twisted by your heart
but the caveat
it was mine all along

april 3 2023 3:36pm

broken by the parts of you,
i found myself in the fire
the flame
the wisdom
brought to you
by spirit handed on a silver platter
of pain
sworn in by faith
i met you to bring me this miracle,
assigning myself here
and that is enough love
to last me
a lifetime

even if it seems unbearable,
it's out of unconditional love.

april 7 2023 9:29pm

you're a loop inside my head
i have on repeat
because not being next to you
will be the death of me

too bad we're strangers
left on read
it's the dragging uncertainty
left inside my head

i'm dying
the quivering
my heart
is shattering

the broken
love bondage
the clear cut crosses

the mindless
come down
of last years
slow drown

the painful
the breaking
of last life's
clearing

i miss you
oh do i
the pain is
all mine

april 7 2023 9:29pm

because i'm broken
without you
but too bad
you never knew

i'm sinking
the floating
oh my minds
exploding

i need you
i feel you
but the pain is
not for you

do you feel me?
it's nothing new
inside me
it's so cruel

i don't understand
how you were the one man
who left my heart sinking
what was i thinking

to let you
in my head
for you to leave me
on fucking read

without you
in my life
it makes me
want to die

april 7 2023 9:29pm

but the feeling
the come down
is worse when
you're not around

i know we'll
never be the same
because you think
this is a game

but i know
it was all real
it was the love struck
that signed the deal

the only good thing
that came from this
is that i found myself
lost nothing else…

grieving your love
that i never had
oh darling
makes me so sad

the feelings i felt
deep in my heart
the creation
of all this art

i channeled
our children
they only hope
to see us win

april 7 2023 9:29pm

but you're too cynical
in all this mess
so i leave it
all to rest

because this come down
it breaks my heart
but luckily
all this art

even your family
understands me
but you can't
seem to believe

that this is perfect
the perfect mess
but you chose
to leave the rest

because it's too hard
for you to mind
that true love
is meant to find

i found it
when i met you
in the summer days
before june

and the magic
of all this mess
is that you left my heart
fearless

april 7 2023 9:29pm

i feel reckless
in loving you
but that's the pain
of being so cruel

because to love something
that's so far
from complete
is such a scarce

because what if
i never knew
what life would be like
without you

                                          i wish to never know,

april 9 2023 10:27am

you were merely a distraction
that's all that happened
to the opening doors
to the closing drawers
of our love sanction
i release you
for my vision is mine
it's all divine
i have trust
i have faith
for heaven's sake
that i'm on the right path
and you were merely there
to guide me home

well i'm home now.

april 16 2023 11:24am

i feel for you
like the sky is blue
and i already knew
the month before june
that you were on your way to me
like the fault in destiny
and like the night is grey
it was never meant to stay

but these simple reminders
remind me
that love always wins

april 16 2023 12:19pm

i feel so much love in my heart
the feeling is overwhelming
to the point of over flow
it feels soft
my inner child fed
she is nourished
and well met
with all her needs
and more
as i walk out the door
i see you
and your inner child
he is soft and smitten
waiting with a single flower
you've been planning this all week
waiting for the perfect moment
the perfect day
the perfect flower
you're waiting to find the perfect flower
to hand to me
on fate's doorstep
but while you're waiting
let me remind you
i don't like perfect
i like fucked up
dismantled
"ugly"
broken
distaster
because it was the broken parts of me
that led me to you
and it wasn't until then
i was able to fix them
so bring me your broken flowers
bring me the uglies
i want nothing more
than to see truth in its flesh

april 16 2023 12:22pm

bring me your broken flowers
the ones you feel small
the ones that are broken
i want them all

i want the uglies
that are too bare to share
it's the broken parts of you
that i can't get enough of

so these flowers represent
love's truest form
because when they come broken
true love can form

april 18 2023 10:38pm

what is it about you
and that summer afternoon
that kept me inside
soul ties

the alchemy of love
is lost, faded
my true heart's desire
gone, jaded

you use to be my muse
i got so use
to you on my mind
all the fucking time

but now that i'm jaded
the fate
it has faded
the chemistry of content
it fills me instead

because in the past you were mine
all the fucking time
every thought and despair
it was you in the air

but now that you're gone
i had to become strong
and lose the sense of denial
in this love sick trial

of faded desire
complete love fire
of burning passion
in soul sunken fashion

april 18 2023 10:38pm

but the reality is
my human match
is that alchemy is chemistry
and our souls
weren't meant to last

in this life time of feelings
staring at ceilings
for this 3d desire
my soul's fueling fire

but on this earth plane
all there is
is pain
because my soul's given wish
resulted in you
being missed

and in the alchemy of time
i wish you were mine
but i give our love to fate
and wait for that destiny day

where you'll meet me at the concert hall
of heaven's door
and all this pain
this gruesome pain
will be worth
worth it all

may 4 2023 7:47pm

your name haunts me
like the writings on your chest
the feelings i surprise
the million reasons why
i must stay

but you're a million miles away

from wanting me
finding peace
sovereignty
it's in the million ways
i wish you'd say
i love you

but you're silent

because words spoken
are too hard to grasp
it's the feelings of love
of ever last
that you're afraid of
and i'm missing you cuz
you're my twin flame
my muse slave

my alchemy
desire
you set my soul
on fire

and these lyrics they must stay
because even tho you're a million miles away
i still
forever
will
love

may 4 2023 7:47pm

whether it's true
or false blue
it's kept me sane
from your million
miles
away

i love you space boy

                                        thank you for the muse
                                            the writing cues
                                              i'll never forget
                                                the day dream
                                                    alchemy
                                            when i met you

                                  thank you times a million

may 18 2023 12:08pm

my poetry is fading
you're not one in the same
do you hear what i'm saying
not anymore
because you walked through the door
the other direction
these feelings affections
are not the same anymore
but the difference between us
is too sure to feel just
we're not one in the same
it's the feeling of pain
that kept me in your game
because as long as i'm feeling

i'm here

it was the part of you
your destiny
that got me feeling like
the best of me
the long chats
the crickets
the feelings
i'm missing
the thoughts in your brain
are driving me insane
because i can't read your mind
were you ever really mine?
no
just the thought of you kills me
the feelings of misery
haunts my brain
and it sounds so vain

to even say this out loud
that i loved you.

may 18 2023 12:08pm

so addicted to the feeling
you made me feel like i never did before
and now those feelings are gone
i'm searching, i'm searching for them
but they are no more
and it kills me

because i close my eyes
and i imagine the times
i felt you
because when i feel you
i feel myself
for the first time
and without you
i lose my god damn mind

i miss you

i miss the feelings,

may 27 2023 11:01pm

i've reached my point
i've reached my limit
where nothing's worth
all this giving

because you're not there
and all this spare
time i have given
but you're left missing…

i'm missing the parts of you
i can't seem to feel the new
because it's all black
it's all black and blue

my wrist are cut
from all this living
my heart and soul
is left with no forgiving

because i thought i knew
from the depths of you
but now i'm left
black and blue

my sheets are shredded
bears beheaded
from all this dread
inside my head

and i can't believe
all this time
i let you get
the best of mine

may 27 2023 11:01pm

how dare you burden
such a sacred space
i've created so ever-lastly
but now it's so badly

i'm scared to be living
with all this pain
the hardest part
i'm the one to blame

you did nothing
but walk into my life
but that was everything
it was the death of mine

your heart was burdened
i could feel it from a depth
read you like a book
i could read the whole set

but with all this time
you're still not mine
and now i'm in pain
and it's driving me
driving me
insane

june 9 2023 6:42pm

my soul whispers through music you'll never
glimmer

    do you hear my calling
        do you hear my calling

                      my soul that ever
whispers
                      my soul
that ever whispers

                      through
    sounds you'll never glimmer

    through sounds you'll never glimmer

        do you hear my calling

            do you hear my calling,

june 11 2023 5:03pm

there's something about the way you move
the way you dance
i just can't
resist the way i feel about you
the feelings they surround you
when i'm surely in your presence

there's something about the way you move
the way you dance
i just can't
get the feeling out my brain
my body surely feels insane
when i'm depleted of you
it's nothing simply short of new

it's the missing piece inside my brain
the reason i sure go insane
when i'm not around you
surely starts to feel blue

it's the brokenness inside my brain
that drowns my heart in shattered pain
when i'm releasing of you
because you're nothing short of new

the agony of misery
the short distance fury
the chemical slurry

of the broken parts of you
they just happen to complete me too…

july 13 2023 5:37pm

i wonder what you're doing
i wonder if it's grand
do you even hear me
i hope you understand

                         the way you looked at me tonight
                         made me think the stars aligned
                                 perfectly in figures
                            i wonder if you hear them

am i crazy to think

         this whole love is hood winked

                      to the dreams that i see

      the things we could be…

it's all too nice
    it's all just right
       it's the feeling
          it's the scenery
             it's the mess
                that's hood winked

                     the message is unclear
                     i wonder of you dear

belong to me
       for eternity
            the rest
               will be
                   complete

if you trust

            hood winked

july 29 2023 9:35am

too much in my head
not enough in my heart
tangled at the seems
connected through the parts

the parts of you
the parts of me
threads forever lasting
threads forever see

see me for myself
see you for you
but once the thread becomes tangled
too much to undo

i'm done from the seems
for though it seems to be
to be forever tangled
what a nightmare beyond belief

because i feel you in my sleep
you're like the ecstasy
i crave forever lonely
i crave forever that might be

forever is too long
but not long enough
to meet you in my dreams
it's a part of the threads complete

complete disbar oh where
oh where it seems to be
enough forever lasting
enough begins to be

to be forever lasting
                        that's the twin flame secrecy

august 15 2023 2:36pm

you play songs about your feelings
but i doubt you for your reasons
they're always stuck inside my head
with the lyrics you never said

i may be new to this
the rhythm of the music
but there's something about the come down
that's coming all around

the wishes are overdue
like the songs and all their queues
the same reason i cry
is because the love songs never lie

i just wish this was you instead.

august 19 2023 1:07pm

ricochet
by your name
the thought that keeps me up at night

and through the night
all the time
you're the lingering thought

because i'm left distraught
from all the haunt
of the last time we spoke

because it was the last time
i felt alive
and all this time
you've been on my mind

ricochet by your name
the hopes of you to stay
with out this haze
of all this craze

created by

                                            the ricochet

august 15 2023 12:07pm

i drop the pieces of you to the fertile ground
where you will flourish through the sound
the sound of my whisper
the sound of my soul
that's where you'll find me
and make us whole

i release these pieces of you
for my own sovereignty

thank you
i love you
delete

december 17 2022 3:14pm

poetic outcast
was the name she gave herself
for missing the meaning in life
without a story to tell

words written on paper
glanced as poetry
the poetic outcast
knew nothing in reality

she watched and wallowed
in ways you couldn't tell
the abundance of commas and markers
was the only true spell

the words she casted on herself
the words she casted on him
the only way to communicate
with the world was from within

she forgot how to speak
only how to write
oh the days of agony
not sleeping at night

without the conversations
made in person
only written words
were the discernment for connection

sadflowerswritten
though these pages were
never meant to be read
they have left my soul fed
with the idea that
maybe i was always
suppose to sing
or to ring
a little sadness in
for you,

the words left unsaid

    feathers that led

        2am threads…

"became the flowers in my head"

laced in the alphabet i strung for myself
to escape to

and now
the whole world can bloom

this is my bloom,
taylor mulholland
xx

- sadflowerswritten -

wildflowers don't bloom without any rain

www.ingramcontent.com/pod-product-compliance
Lightning Source LLC
Chambersburg PA
CBHW051123160426
43195CB00014B/2315